THE NO-FLY ZONE

Keeping The Invasion Of The Enemy
OUT OF YOUR HOUSE!

HANK KUNNEMAN

Copyright © 2019 – Hank Kunneman
One Voice Ministries
All rights reserved. This book is protected by the copyright laws of the United States of America. This book may not be copied or reprinted for commercial gain or profit. The use of short quotations or occasional page copying for personal or group study is permitted and encouraged. Permission will be granted upon request.

Unless otherwise identified, Scripture quotations are from the King James Version of the Bible. Copyright © 1979, 1980, 1982 by Thomas Nelson, Inc., publishers. Used by permission.

Strong, James. The New Strong's Exhaustive Concordance of the Bible. Nashville, TN: Thomas Nelson, 1991.

One Voice Ministries
P.O. Box 390460
Omaha, NE 68139
855-777-7907
www.hankandbrenda.org

The No-Fly Zone, *Keeping the Invasion of the Enemy Out of Your House*
ISBN 978-0-9970645-9-9

TABLE OF CONTENTS

Chapter 1	Your House is Set Apart as a No-fly Zone!
Chapter 2	By No Means Shall Anything Harm You
Chapter 3	Setting Your Standard
Chapter 4	Stand Your Ground!

Dedication

This writing is dedicated to my spiritual son in the faith, Dodji Salifou, who has made it his mission to pray for me fervently. He was the first person I heard command the enemy's efforts against me, my family, and ministry to fall and while commanding demonic spirits, he would declare, "This is a no-fly zone!" That revelation became concrete in my spirit and it was that declaration that caused this book to be birthed.

CHAPTER ONE
Your House is Set Apart as a No-fly Zone!

And I will sever in that day the land of Goshen, in which my people dwell, that no swarms of flies shall be there; to the end thou mayest know that I am the LORD in the midst of the earth (Exodus 8:22).

One of the greatest stories in the Bible, the deliverance of the children of Israel from Egypt, gives us tremendous insight into what it means to live in a "no-fly zone." God's intent for us as believers is that we experience His provision and protection in the same way the children of Israel did during the plagues in Egypt. The same Lord who was in their midst is also in our midst, and He enables us to stand against anything the enemy would send to harm us.

When God sent the first two of ten plagues that would ultimately cause His people to be delivered, they began with

Pharaoh's magicians being able to emulate the plagues being brought by Moses (see Exodus 7-8). However, even before the ten famous plagues were enacted, Pharaoh's magicians were able to turn their rods into serpents just as Moses did (see Ex. 7:12). Since his sorcerers were able to do exactly what Moses did, Pharaoh was unmoved by this supernatural occurrence. As a result of Pharaoh's resistance to God, the series of plagues begins to follow, but just like the turning of rods to serpents, the sorcerers were again able to emulate what Moses did. Thus, the first two plagues had little effect on Pharaoh.

First, the magicians matched the plague of blood in the water. *"And the magicians of Egypt did so with their enchantments: and Pharaoh's heart was hardened, neither did he hearken unto them; as the LORD had said"* (Exodus 7:22). Following this first plague, they matched the plague of frogs. *And the magicians did so with their enchantments, and brought up frogs upon the land of Egypt* (Exodus 8:7).

While these workers of evil were able to precisely match both plagues, the Bible doesn't say how this was visibly obvious to Pharaoh or other onlookers. When Moses' rod turned the water to blood, the blood filled every river, pond, stream, and even all their drinking vessels. It seems it would have been difficult to differentiate between the blood that came from Moses' rod and that which came from the enchantments of the magicians. Similarly, with the frogs being in such abundance, how would one know which frogs God and Moses produced and which ones the magicians conjured up?

Again, the Bible doesn't say this, but is it possible that as a form of retaliation, Pharaoh's magicians exacted some of these same plagues on the places where the children of Israel lived within the land of Egypt? Maybe. We don't know for sure, but if that *were* to have been the case, Pharaoh would have likely assumed that his magicians had been very successful and believed these two first plagues were simple magic tricks and nothing to be alarmed about. We don't know for sure, but it is something to consider.

While the Bible doesn't say the magicians were able to bring frogs into the homes or properties of the children of Israel, it does say they were able to emulate these two plagues in an obvious visible manner. Certainly the Israelite slaves working in Egypt were initially affected by these two events. We know this because the Scripture says that the *entire land* was filled with a stench from the blood and frogs (see Ex. 7:21; 8:14). Undoubtedly, the Israelite slaves were tasked with cleanup from the mess created and that alone would have affected them immensely.

What we *can* fairly conclude is that at that moment, it seemed that the workers of evil were able to keep pace with and match the power of God, and the horror of what was happening did affect the children of Israel. They weren't fully removed from the effect of the plagues at this point.

This is important to consider because many times we can look around at life, society, and the current culture and realize we live amid much evil that seems to abound. It can appear as though the workers of darkness have an upper hand against God's people as wickedness continues to rise. At a glance, it might seem like evil is overcoming good, rather than the other way around.

Perhaps in your own life it seems the enemy has had some sort of advantage. Maybe it is in relation to your health, finances, or an issue in your family. It seems like the trial at hand is never going to be overcome. It feels like the power of God is not having any effect on that difficult situation and every time you gain a victory, it seems the enemy comes in with a counter assault.

Let's consider that this is how Moses and the children of Israel may have felt in Egypt at first. Here was Moses' grand opening to confront Pharaoh with a great plague, and a great plague it was! However, imagine what Moses and Aaron may have thought as they were standing there and, through demonic power, the evil magicians were able to copy what just happened. For a moment, put yourself in their shoes. Most of us would have been stunned and may have felt this big supernatural moment wasn't so special, since it didn't outdo or put to silence the workers of evil.

It may appear that the enemy has an upper hand in many areas in society right now. It may seem in your own life like the attacks of the evil one aren't being overcome. Nevertheless, be encouraged, because just as happened with the children of Israel in Egypt, everything is about to shift in your favor!

The Day of Difference

After the plagues of blood and frogs concluded, Pharaoh's heart was hardened and he wouldn't relent from holding his grip on the children of Israel. The next plague that came upon Egypt was the plague of lice. Again, the magicians used their enchantments to try and emulate the plague. However, they were about to realize that something had suddenly shifted!

And the magicians did so with their enchantments to bring forth lice, but they could not: so there were lice upon man, and upon beast (Exodus 8:18).

This time the magicians were powerless! The Bible says, *"but they could not"* (Ex. 8:18). They couldn't mimic the display of God's power. They were so overcome that they were forced to report their failure to Pharaoh and acknowledge that what was happening this time was, in fact, the finger of God!

Make no mistake about it, when the finger of God comes on the scene, the devil and workers of evil don't stand a chance! We are in a prophetic season where we are going to see the finger of God touch certain situations and paralyze the enemy's efforts! There is coming a day and a new prophetic era where the finger of God is going to move and we will be given the obvious upper hand of favor. Believe this in faith over your own life, too!

The day when the plague of lice came upon Egypt was the day of difference, when God began to set apart the houses and lives of the children of Israel from the Egyptians. A visible separation was beginning to take place. Of course, I do not believe the lice came upon the children of Israel, but at the same time, the Bible does not clarify a full separation of God's people from the Egyptians at this point. It only says the magicians couldn't mimic the plague (see Ex. 8). By the next plague, the swarms of flies, the difference becomes very distinct.

The No-Fly Zone!

The next morning, God tells Moses to visit Pharaoh and demand that he let God's people go (see Ex. 8:20). God informs Moses that the next plague will be swarms of flies. The word *flies* in Exodus 8:21 doesn't not appear in the original manuscript, so the real meaning is that it was swarms of various flying insects, and probably not just the typical house fly we are accustomed to seeing. Research indicates that many of these "flies" were stinging or biting insects. The Amplified version of Exodus 8:21 describes these flies as "bloodsucking gadflies." Gadflies includes various forms of flies such at the botfly that are particularly awful for humans. Botflies lay their eggs on the female mosquito which, in turn, transfers those eggs into the flesh of the person bitten. The result is the botfly larvae grow inside the person, causing great pain and possible infection. In modern medicine, the removal of botfly larvae must usually be removed through surgery. Botflies are also harmful to livestock as well.[1]

Of course, that is just one possibility and it's likely there were several species of stinging insects and pests in the mix. Imagine how terrible these swarms must have been! But it was on this particular day when the swarms came into the land, that God made a defining statement in Exodus 8:22-23:

"And I will sever in that day the land of Goshen, in which my people dwell, that no swarms of flies shall be there; to the end thou mayest know that I am the Lord in the midst of the earth. And I will put a division between my people and they people: tomorrow shall this sign be."

The Amplified translation of these verses says, *"I will sever and set the land of Goshen apart."* The New International Version uses the phrase, *"I will deal differently with the land of Goshen,"* and *"I will make a distinction between my people and your people."* God was making it clear that the land and homes of His people were going to be distinctly different from those of the Egyptians. What a day of difference it was as the flies descended on the Egyptians, but not one fly could touch the children of Israel. God's people were living in a no-fly zone!

Your House is Set Apart

Like the children of Israel, our homes are to be free of the enemy's invasion. Our homes and lives are to be no-fly zones to the swarms of demons we see coming on society, culture, and the earth. Throughout Scripture, God has always had a protection plan for His people and now in Christ we are told to resist the works of the enemy and when we do that, he will be forced to flee (see James 4:7).

Notice there were swarms of flies specifically inside the *houses* of the Egyptians, but no flies could enter the homes of the children of Israel. This reveals that God put up a barrier that made their property off limits to the flies. The Bible calls satan "Beelzebub," which means "the lord of the flies" (see Mk. 3:22).2 Flies speak of demons, and the flies that invaded Egypt were a depiction of the demonic invasion that had entered all their homes.

I believe the decade of 2020-2030 will be a decade of difference where we will see God bring a divine separation between His people and those of the world. It will be a time for the Church to be exonerated across the globe. Thus, we will see many situations in which the invasions of demons will be paralyzed, causing certain territories and parts of culture to become literal "no-fly zones." That doesn't mean the spirit of anti-Christ that seeks to persecute the Church will disappear; our Lord Jesus could return at any moment. In this coming decade, however, there will be a great awakening that will uplift the Name of Jesus in an undeniable way that the enemy will not be able to stop. There will be a great distinction between those who are on the Lord's side and those who are not.

Just like in Goshen, know that your home, life, and property are all off-limits to the devil! See your house as a no-fly zone that the enemy is not allowed to enter. God has put up a barrier and satan and his swarms of demons cannot touch you, your property, or your family. God's finger is bringing a divine separation and He is making a difference in all that concerns you. Your house has been set apart and you live in a no-fly zone!

ENDNOTES

1. See https://en.wikipedia.org/wiki/Warble_fly; https://health.howstuffworks.com/skin-care/problems/medical/skin-parasite7.htm.

2. James Strong, The New Strong's Exhaustive Concordance of the Bible (Nashville, TN: Thomas Nelson, 1991), Hebrew #1176.

CHAPTER TWO
By No Means Shall Anything Harm You

Behold, I give unto you power to tread on serpents and scorpions, and over all the power of the enemy: and nothing shall by any means hurt you (Luke 10:19).

As born-again believers filled with the Holy Spirit, we have been given power to overcome the works of the devil. We often quote the part of Luke 10:19 that talks about having the authority to tread on the power of the enemy, but we often neglect to quote the last phrase of the verse which says, "nothing shall by any means hurt you." This means that there is not any method of harm the devil can use against you.

When the Egyptians were being invaded by flies, the children of Israel were nearby. It's not clear as to whether the people of God were able to fully witness these swarms from a distance and see what terrible effect they were having on their Egyptian neighbors. It's reasonable to think they did see the swarms, and perhaps they wondered if at some point the pestilence would come on them, too. Remember, the Israelites were just beginning to encounter this man Moses and the acts he was suddenly performing. We don't know all of what might have been going through the minds of God's people initially. Maybe they wondered if the flies would attack their houses. It's certainly reasonable to think so.

We can also safely believe that instinctively by nature, the flies would have attempted to cross over into Goshen, but they couldn't do so because there was a supernatural barrier there. Consider what it would have been like to be one of the Israelites hearing the cries of the afflicted Egyptians or seeing the skies filled with insects off in the distance. Imagine what went through their minds as they saw the later plague of devastating hail approaching on the skyline. Think of a time where you saw a dangerous storm in the distance and how you felt. The people in Goshen surely had to wonder if they would remain safe. But I'm sure after realizing the swarms couldn't cross over, and each time a new plague came that didn't enter their dwelling, the children of Israel eventually learned there wasn't a method of evil that could harm them! Eventually they would have known that nothing could touch them--not flies, locusts, boils, hail, darkness, or death! They were immune!

We Have Supernatural Immunity

Think for a moment of all the methods the enemy tries to use to attack us. We could list sickness, infirmity, financial lack, family problems, mental and emotional struggles, and even things that happen in the daily business of life that come to challenge our well-being. Of course, we live in a fallen world and the curse of evil is everywhere, much like it was when the children of Israel were in the midst of the evil falling upon the Egyptians. They were surrounded by evil, yet they remained protected from it. While the enemy may be raging all around and may try to bring some attack of evil against your life, know that Jesus made it clear that you have immunity. Attacks may try to come against you and even try to make you feel miserable or worried about the outcome, but the methods the enemy is using are powerless. More than that, it's illegal because we have been granted a supernatural immunity from Jesus that says, *"by no means shall anything harm you"* (Luke 10:19). This doesn't mean the enemy won't try, but he's not allowed to inflict harm and devastation upon your life.

Perhaps the reason that many of God's people are being attacked by sickness, lack, and other things is because we haven't fully received the revelation that we have been granted supernatural immunity. Similar to the children of Israel who had to witness the plagues all around them and come to the realization they couldn't be touched, we also have to realize we cannot be touched.

What might happen if we got this revelation? Rather than fearing the latest disease being announced on television or the internet, or fearing some national or global recession, we would immediately know that although the plague is nearby, it cannot harm us. Like the Israelites, we may feel the effects of these things around us, but we must be assured they cannot bring us harm. This is called walking in faith. It's having the confidence and assurance that God will deliver us from evil and keep us safe.

Too many believers worry in the back of their minds if they will be affected by some attack in life, or if they will make it through. This is a picture of the children of Israel being focused on Egypt and what is happening there, rather than focusing on the blessing that was in Goshen. I want to encourage you not to get caught up in being focused on the present "plagues of Egypt" we see happening in our world today. We need to stop reading about them so much, researching them, and talking as if they might come upon us. Don't get out of your Goshen! What do I mean by that? I am saying, don't leave your place of faith and confidence that God is your Protector and Shield. Keep your attention on His promises and His Word. Your Goshen is your place of supernatural immunity and your place of knowing that you shall be delivered from the evil all around!

Remember Psalm 91, which is a chapter that we often quote regarding God's protection. We could call it the chapter of supernatural immunity! Look here specifically at verses 7-10:

A thousand shall fall at thy side, and ten thousand at thy right hand; but it shall not come nigh thee. Only with thine eyes shalt thou behold and see the reward of the wicked. Because thou hast made the Lord, which is my refuge, even the most High, thy habitation; There shall no evil befall thee, neither shall any plague come nigh thy dwelling.

These verses describe supernatural immunity. Like the children of Israel, you may be able to witness what is going on in your "Egypt." They surely witnessed others around them falling by the thousands at their right hand and they saw the reward of the wicked coming upon the Egyptians, but it didn't come near them! They could stand confidently and safely in Goshen, where no plague was able to enter.

You might be feeling today like you are suffering from a plague of sorts. Step back into Goshen in your thoughts and attitudes. Remove yourself from focusing on the plague of Egypt, so to speak. The reason many of us suffer is because we get caught up in "living in Egypt" when it comes to our circumstances. Again, we do this when we continue focus on what's happening in Egypt rather than seeing all the blessings in Goshen. We can't let this type of fear saturate our thoughts. Instead, we must get back into Goshen where we are supernaturally immune.

I remember years ago when we first moved into our house. It was a newly constructed neighborhood and as houses were going up around ours, there were some grading issues on several of the lots nearby causing some water runoff that wasn't being properly drained between the new homes. Our house was on one of the lower lots, so all the water wanted to run in our direction. One of the houses being built nearby kept having flood issues in the basement. However, my wife kept standing outside our house and declaring, "No flooding can happen in Goshen!" Of course, since our house was among the lowest, it would have been the likely place for the water to go. But she just kept proclaiming protection, and out of all the houses there, we never had any water coming in during that building phase! Praise God, the grading issues eventually got fixed, but to this day we have been immune to that issue.

What am I saying? You can do the same thing! Claim your supernatural immunity from disaster! Stand up and claim that no evil can touch you in Goshen and there is no method of evil that can harm or injure you. We have to stand in this authority, just like the children of Israel had to stay in Goshen. Stay out of Egypt by refusing fear and worry. Stay out of Egypt by not speaking and receiving curses or plagues in your life!

Let's look at the specific plagues that came upon the Egyptians and see how each of them can prophetically represents something for which Jesus has provided us supernatural immunity.

The plague on the water: turned to blood.
This first plague represents Jesus' coming to give us the uncorruptible water of eternal life. It also speaks of blessing on our physical food and drink. God said He would bless our bread and water (see Ex. 23:25) and Jesus said our heavenly Father would see to it that our food and water is always provided (see Mt. 7:25-34).

The plague of frogs.
The frogs speak of bondage, strongholds or addictions. When

Moses asked Pharaoh when he wanted the plague of frogs lifted, Pharaoh said, "Tomorrow" (see Ex. 8:9-10). Pharaoh was shockingly willing to keep the frogs for one more day! This speaks of the things we struggle to be free from. But remember, Jesus said He came to deliver the captives who are bound and set them free! (see Luke 4:18).

The plague of lice.
Since we know that lice typically affect a person's head, we can think of the plague of lice as mental and emotional oppression. We can be delivered from mental illnesses and issues such as depression, memory problems, mind-altering conditions, and a host of things that can affect our minds. We can be free from these things because, through Jesus, we have been given the mind of Christ (see 1 Cor. 2:16).

The swarms of flies.
The swarms are a picture of demonic attacks and onslaughts. Psalm 91:5 says we should not be afraid of the arrow that flies. The insects that flew in against the Egyptians are like the fiery arrows or darts of the wicked one and his demons (see Eph. 6:16). We have authority over the devil because Jesus has redeemed us from the curse (see Gal. 3:13).

The death of the cattle.
When all the cattle and livestock of Egypt died, it represented the loss of their livelihood, their personal property, and their possessions. During the plague, everything they owned was unprotected. In Christ, we have received divine protection from the evil one (see 2 Thess. 3:3).

The plague of boils.
Obviously, the plague of boils speaks of sickness, infirmity, and other physical ailments. Jesus is our Healer and by His stripes we are healed (see Is. 53:4-5, Mt. 8:17; 1 Pet. 2:24).

The plague of darkness.
Darkness depicts spiritual blindness and a lack of revelation. The Bible says during this plague the Egyptians could not see each other (see Ex. 10:23). They were essentially blind. Darkness also evokes fear and terror, but Jesus came to give us light and deliver us from all manner of fear (see Eph. 5:14; 2 Tim. 1:7).

The plague of hail.
Hail is a picture of the storms of life. Just as Jesus delivered the disciples from storms and the Apostle Paul was spared from storms, we can trust that Jesus will deliver us from life's storms and not allow us to be tested beyond what we can bear (see 1 Cor. 10:13).

The plague of locusts.
The Bible reveals that the army of locusts that came on the Egyptians devoured everything that was left after the plague of hail (see Ex. 10:15). Scripture uses locusts to portray lack and devastation, but we have the promise that Jesus came to give us life that is filled with abundance and free from lack (see Jn. 10:10).

The death of the firstborn.
The death of all the firstborn of Egypt is a well-known picture

of our salvation. We have been "passed over" by the curse of death because we are covered by the blood of Jesus. But this also represents our promise of long life and deliverance from premature death! (see Ps. 91:16).

These ten plagues paint a wonderful picture of how Jesus has made provision to deliver us in the same way He delivered the children of Israel. Trust today in the fact that Jesus has given you supernatural immunity in your life. When we carry this revelation, we can be confident that we have power over the enemy and that there is not any mean or method he can bring to invade our lives or houses!

CHAPTER THREE
Setting Your Standard

...Let my people go, that they may serve me (Exodus 9:1).

Moses' repeated message to Pharaoh was to let God's people be released so they could be free to serve God. The key point of them being delivered was so the people could serve God with a full heart of purity and dedication. They were being delivered from slavery so they could dedicate their lives and homes to the worship of Jehovah. Goshen being a "no-fly zone" was a depiction of their homes and lives in the promised land being free from demonic influence and invasion.

Not only are our homes and lives meant to be free from demonic invasion by way of attack and mayhem, they are to be places where the Spirit of God rules and reigns. Our houses and lives are to be holy. God wanted the children of Israel to be free so they would build their lives around Him. His desire was that everything they owned and all they did would reflect their worship of Him. This is also what God wants for us. He wants to be the very essence of our homes and our lives.

Joshua 24:15 says, *"choose you this day whom ye will serve; whether the gods which your fathers served that were on the other side of the flood, or the gods of the Amorites, in whose land ye dwell: but as for me and my house, we will serve the Lord."*

This well-known verse describes the intent of God for the children of Israel, whom He had called out of Egypt to serve Him. So many times, after they'd been delivered from Egypt, the children of Israel returned to idolatry and allowed their homes to be contaminated with sin, darkness, and evil. And many years later under Joshua's leadership, we still see God's people having to be admonished to set their lives and homes apart in service and reverence to the Lord. Over and over, because they did not do this, destruction and tragedy were able to invade their houses.

If we want our homes to be no-fly zones, we need to ensure we are setting ourselves apart in service to the Lord. It is critical that we set a holy standard in our homes. Remember that demons are attracted to filth. They hang around where there is a stench, just like flies are attracted to the smell of garbage and waste. If we want our houses to be no-fly zones, we need to cleanse them of any filth that is displeasing to the Lord.

The world is full of evil and sinful things that we can allow to invade our homes if we are not careful. We are well of aware of how our society is saturated with promiscuity, witchcraft, carnality, and wickedness. Even some things that seem innocent enough can still have the world's corruption upon them. Modern media allows easy access for compromise to enter our lives. Consider that so much of what we see and hear is packaged in a very palatable way and, if we aren't careful, we can be easily deceived into allowing things to enter and contaminate our lives.

In Matthew 24, one of the key things Jesus repeatedly warned about regarding the last days was that we be careful not to be deceived. Deception among God's people is on the rise and can affect us just like the children of Israel were affected when they left Egypt. Scripture gives us a clear admonition, comparing us to the children of Israel in the wilderness:

But with many of them God was not well pleased: for they were overthrown in the wilderness. Now these things were our examples, to the intent we should not lust after evil things, as they also lusted (1 Corinthians 10:5-6).

Instead of keeping their lives and homes clean, the children of Israel allowed an infiltration of evil that caused them to sin. Instead of their journey through the wilderness being a continuation of the no-fly zone of Goshen, they allowed pestilence to infiltrate and at one point, they were attacked by serpents (see 1 Cor. 9-10). The entire chapter of 1 Corinthians 10 is a comparison of the children of Israel to us as believers and warns us not to get entangled in the things that would pollute our relationship to God.

I believe in the current era, we as God's people, need to be more careful than ever about our choices of entertainment, news, and recreational activities. So many accepted pastimes today are filled with things that break down our holy standard and deviate from the purity of Christ. Things like television and the internet are mediums that not only carry information but can infiltrate our minds and the atmosphere of our homes, polluting our pure relationship with the Lord. We need to set a clear standard about what we will and will not allow, if we want to live in a no-fly zone!

A Different Standard

To live in the no-fly zone that repels the attraction of evil spirits, we need to set a standard that is visibly different from that of the world. Today, many believers are trying to "be relevant" to the culture rather than stand out from the culture. I am not saying that relevance has no place in reaching people. We need to understand the key issues and challenges that form and affect society and show compassion to people. However, under *no circumstance* does Scripture endorse us acting or looking like the world, emulating compromising cultural practices, or accepting lifestyles that God undeniably rejects, in order to "reach the world." In fact, the Word of God admonishes us to set a completely different standard and separate ourselves from the practices of this world.

Wherefore come out from among them, and be ye separate, saith the Lord, and touch not the unclean thing; and I will receive you (2 Corinthians 6:17).

Paul explained to the Church at Corinth that they were to separate themselves from the commonly accepted idols of the day. They were to have a clear and different standard in their homes and lives. We are also called by God to separate ourselves from the common forms of modern idolatry.
I think if we are honest with ourselves, we can all make a mental list of the things we see in our culture that we know the Bible does not endorse. Rather than spend so much time, as many Christians do, reasoning why certain things are acceptable to participate in, let's spend more time knowing how God wants us to be set apart and different. We are not called to look like the world. Let's investigate the many things the Word of God tells us to avoid in order to protect us, so we can keep the flies out of our houses!

Sweep Your House Clean

Jesus taught a powerful principle about setting our standard and keeping our house swept clean so it's always a no-fly zone. In Luke 11:14-26, after He was accused by some people that He was casting out demons through demonic power, Jesus goes on to say that no kingdom divided against itself can stand. In other words, you can't mix God's power with demonic influence. He explained that one will eventually neutralize the other. In verse 23, Jesus expresses that those who are for Him cannot have a divided way of thinking. They need to be fully for Him in an uncompromising way. He then uses the example of sweeping your house clean from demonic influence, in the context of casting out demons. From this same teaching, let's look at the example found in Matthew 12:43-45 in the New

Living Translation:

"When an evil spirit leaves a person, it goes into the desert, seeking rest but finding none. Then it says, 'I will return to the person I came from.' So it returns and finds its former home empty, swept, and in order. Then the spirit finds seven other spirits more evil than itself, and they all enter the person and live there. And so that person is worse off than before. That will be the experience of this evil generation."

Jesus says that a person can remove the influence of demons from their life and household, but if it's left empty, eventually the influence of evil will find its way back. Demons are always looking for an inroad. They will seek any opportunity to gain entrance. How do we keep them from gaining access?

First, we need to remove the things in our lives and homes that attract these evil spirits. Once we do that, we need to fill our lives with things that attract the presence of God. Demons can't enter a house that is clean and then, in turn, is filled with the glory of the Lord. This applies to your personal life as well as your physical home. The key is to remove the things that attract demonic flies and then fill your house and life with things the invite the Holy Spirit. When these two factors are in play, demons may try and seek an entrance, but because the house is full of the presence of the Lord, they have no access.

If you want to live in a no-fly zone, sweep your house clean. Make some decisions about what you are going to read and review on TV or online. Decide what types of entertainment are not going to be allowed in your home. Determine where you stand regarding your own walk with God and lifestyle in the current culture. Make sure your home is not an environment of strife and that you are making every effort to walk in love. After you determine what is not allowed, then fill your home and life with the things of God. Fill your house with worship, the Word of God, and things that create an atmosphere for the anointing. Determine to set a standard in your life and home that you will not alter or allow to be compromised. Setting your godly standard will repel evil spirits and cause your life and home to be a no-fly zone!

CHAPTER FOUR
Stand Your Ground!

Wherefore take unto you the whole armour of God, that ye may be able to withstand in the evil day, and having done all, to stand (Ephesians 6:13).

Now we are aware that God wants our lives and homes to be a no-fly zone for the enemy, and we've outlined some ways to set a standard that allows God to rule and reign in our lives. In this chapter, I want to give some further practical keys that you can use to establish your house as a no-fly zone and continually defend your life against the invasion of the enemy. The Bible teaches us in Ephesians 6:13 that we are to take a firm stand against the enemy. It says, *"having done all to stand."* This reveals that standing our ground against the enemy it is not just a one-time event. It is an ongoing offensive stance that we must take regularly if we want to overcome the forces of darkness. It's something we need to continuously keep established, not only on days when we feel attacked. We need to do it when it seems everything is perfect and there is no imminent threat. Military forces don't just establish lines of security when they are under attack, they establish them every day to ensure that the boundaries lines are secure and intact.

Let's cover five of the most important things we can do to establish our houses as no-fly zones. These are things my wife and I do regularly in our own home because, like you, we want to keep the invasion of the enemy out!

Take God at His Word

Of course, we can't establish a no-fly zone if we don't know what the Scriptures say. Develop a working knowledge of God's Word and keep it continually in your heart. In modern culture, I see more and more good-hearted and well-meaning believers faltering because they don't know the Word of God. They can't take God at His Word because they simply don't know what He has said! Additionally, there are also veteran believers who "know" the Bible but have allowed it to grow stale. They aren't keeping His Word fresh before them each day, perhaps like they had in the past, and are only relying on what they previously memorized.

God told the children of Israel in the wilderness that they were to gather the manna from heaven every single day. If they neglected to do that and saved some of the manna for the next day, it would rot and turn to worms (see Ex. 16). God was making the point that we need fresh "manna" or food from heaven every day, and we get that by daily meditation in the

Word of God.

In addition to time reading or studying the Word, we also need to speak the Word. Find key Scriptures regarding your life and home and speak them aloud in your house! In Joshua 1:8, the Lord told Joshua to meditate in the law (Word of God) day and night. One of the elements of meditation includes speaking. That could be repeating something under your breath as you lay down to sleep, or it could be a bold declaration spoken through the house. The key is to be in God's Word and speak God's Word. If you don't, eventually the enemy will slowly chip away at your confidence in what God has said. Spoken words are very powerful and necessary tools in standing your ground against the enemy.

Finally, take God at His Word. If He has said something, believe it! Don't look for all the reasons why it doesn't apply to you or conclude that somehow all the miraculous stories in Scripture were for another time in history. Some people also get too concerned about whether they are understanding the Bible correctly, so they are distracted from or dismiss many of God's wonderful promises. Now I am not saying we carelessly misinterpret the Bible; we most certainly need correct doctrine. However, God also knows we are all progressively learning to understand and interpret the Scriptures. I am saying that we should apply the Scriptures without hesitation as best as we can understand them.

Many years ago, I heard the story of a man who was believing to be healed of a heart condition. He began to speak Psalm

57:7 which says, *"My heart is fixed, O God, my heart is fixed."* He used this verse to believe his heart problem would be healed by God. In the proper context of Scripture, this verse isn't actually referring to heart disease. Various translations show that what the Psalmist was saying was that his heart was steadfast, or *fixated* on, the Lord. It was an expression of heartfelt commitment. Yet this gentleman, not fully understanding this, simply stood on this Scripture to believe his heart condition was healed! Even though he mildly misinterpreted the verse, countless Scriptures do promise physical healing. So, in childlike faith, he believed on that verse for his healing from heart disease and was miraculously healed.

I am certainly not advocating taking Scripture out of context, but I do want to point out that we shouldn't overanalyze everything until we talk ourselves out of our blessings. God is pleased when we have simple faith, faith that is quick to believe what He says and run with it. Take God at His Word. Believe it and speak it to establish your house as a no-fly zone!

Take Your Rightful Place of Authority

Another important key is to take the authority Jesus has given and use it! The Bible says, *"Resist the devil and he will flee from you"* (James 4:7). There are many ways we resist the enemy and keep the flies away, but one very important way is by our verbal command. Commanding the devil to leave and stay out is very important. Not only does your command remind you to keep your home secure and not let anything creep in, it's an announcement to the forces of darkness that they can't operate where you live. It's a direct order against them to cease and desist from any works they may attempt.

Take time to stand in your home and announce it as a no-fly zone. This is something my wife and I do on a regular basis. We walk the house, even looking out our windows around our yard, and we decree that no invader or intruder, whether natural or spiritual, is allowed to cross our property lines. We declare that *all* mischief, mayhem, tragedy, and calamity are bound in the Name of Jesus! We formally decree that our house is a no-fly zone! What are we doing when we do this? We are establishing the perimeter through our declaration and taking our rightful authority in Christ.

Countless Scriptures teach us the importance of verbally commanding the devil to leave. We see Jesus do this all throughout His life and ministry. We also see the early apostles do the same thing. They made a practice of commanding evil spirits to leave in the Name of Jesus.

Let's look closer at James 4:7: *"Resist the devil, and he will flee from you."* The word "resist" here means to take an upright and active stance or to stand against. It means to oppose.1 Think for a moment about how you oppose things in life. You don't oppose them by just inwardly thinking about what you aren't going to agree and align with. You typically verbalize your opinion and position on the matter. This is the same way we need to deal with the enemy. We can't just think about removing him. We need to speak and command it! This how we take authority and establish the perimeter. When we do that, the result is that the devil and his demons must flee!

Anoint Your House with Oil

Another thing my wife and I always do is anoint our house with oil. Your house or household includes your home, vehicles and even the members of your family. At the beginning of each new year, we anoint each other and our entire family with oil. We do this to establish the hedge of protection upon our home and our lives for the year, and we do it at other times throughout the year as well.

The Bible says in Isaiah 10:27 that the yoke, which signifies a burden or bondage, shall be destroyed because of the anointing oil. Anointing with oil is powerful in setting a hedge of protection against the enemy!

...and the yoke shall be destroyed because of the anointing oil (Isaiah 10:27 MEV).

What caused the yoke or burden to be destroyed? It was the anointing oil! One of the most unique elements God instituted among the children of Israel was the oil of anointing (see Ex. 30). It was to be a sweet perfume of the aroma and presence of God that would sanctify not only them personally in various situations, but also all the vessels of the sanctuary and all things considered holy. God gives instruction in Exodus 40:9 that all the temple furnishings were to be anointed with oil:

Then you shall take the anointing oil and anoint the tabernacle and all that is in it, and shall consecrate it and all its furnishings; and it shall be holy.

All the physical property of the temple was to be anointed with oil. Anointing with oil is a practice that continued in the New Testament under Christ, so there is no reason we cannot anoint our property with oil in the same way the priests did, to consecrate our homes by faith. We are the priests of our homes, so to speak. The oil represents the presence and power of the Holy Spirit. It is a point of contact where we set things apart as holy or consecrated to God. The book of James teaches that elders are to anoint with oil those who want to be healed (see James 5:14). The disciples also ministered to the sick by anointing them with oil (see Mk. 6:13). This was a sign that the sick were being set apart in consecration to be healed.

Stand your ground by utilizing the practice of anointing with oil. When you do, it's a statement to the forces of darkness that these things are consecrated, holy, and covered in the power of the Holy Spirit.

Apply the Blood of Jesus by Faith

The children of Israel were finally delivered from Egypt after the tenth and final plague, which was the death of the firstborn. On that fateful night for the Egyptians, the children of Israel were instructed by the Lord to put the blood of a lamb on the doorposts of their homes. We know that the lamb's blood was a type and shadow of the blood of Jesus. While they applied it naturally, we apply it by faith. One of the key ways we apply faith is again, by declaration. Jesus taught the power of words and He said we can have what we say (see Mk. 11:23). If we know that the blood of Jesus provides protection, we should be declaring that truth and promise over our lives and homes!

Walk through your home and regularly declare that it is protected by the blood of Jesus. Proclaim that no spirit of death can enter. Not only does the declaration of Jesus' powerful blood repel demons, but it builds your faith in what Jesus made available through His blood. Just as it did for the children of Israel, the blood has made your house a no-fly zone to the powers of darkness!

Do a Regular Review

The last key I want to give you is that you do a regular review of your life and house. The Bible says we are to examine ourselves. Let's look at the first part of 2 Corinthians 13:5:

Examine yourselves, whether ye be in the faith; prove your own selves.

Undoubtedly, this Scripture is telling us to do a regular review. That not only includes a personal examination of our hearts and motives, but it also includes a review of the things we may have unknowingly or unintentionally allowed in our homes. Take time now and then to determine if you have allowed things to creep in that are not pleasing to God. We certainly aren't called to live under condemnation and legalism, but we are called upon by God to review our choices, lives, and motives. Every believer can take steps backward if they are not careful, so we need to stay on the alert.

1 Peter 5:8 says, *"Be sober, be vigilant; because your adversary the devil, as a roaring lion, walketh about, seeking whom he may devour."* The enemy is always on the prowl looking for an entrance. He will certainly try to enter illegally *even if* you don't open a door. That is what thieves and robbers do - they come in uninvited. However, we certainly don't want to be inadvertently giving him free access. Ask the Lord to reveal any areas that you need to shore up. God will be faithful to show any of these areas as needed. Secondly, fix the things you know need to be addressed. Don't delay and hold off for another day. The longer we don't deal with things, the more the enemy is going to find a little hole through which to send his flies. It's like a little tear in your screen door: it might just be a little hole, but that tear is usually just enough to let some bugs in!

Now in saying this, I want to clarify that this doesn't mean we need to live in fear, wondering if we have left some open door to the enemy. I do emphatically believe God covers for us when are ignorant in a certain area, and again, the Holy Spirit is faithful to show us open doors when we ask Him. However, we also need to grow in our spiritual maturity and understanding so we are well aware of the kinds of things that give the devil access and the things we need to change. A regular review of these things will keep our house free from the flies of the devil!

I believe God wants the home and life of every believer to be a no-fly zone. God has promised we can live free. Just like He caused the children of Israel to live under His protection in a no-fly zone, we can have this same experience! Their story is a picture of what Jesus provided for us. Know today that the devil has no method or means to harm you. Build your faith in this promise! Then, as you set a standard for your house and apply the key things necessary to stand your ground, you will know with assurance that you truly live in a no-fly zone!

ENDNOTES

1. James Strong, The New Strong's Exhaustive Concordance of the Bible (Nashville, TN: Thomas Nelson, 1991), Greek #436.

HANK+BRENDA

For more books and resources from
Hank and Brenda Kunneman,
visit us online at HankandBrenda.org

One Voice Ministries
P.O. Box 390460
Omaha, NE 68139
855-777-7907